not a guide to

Durham

Chris Daniel

First published 2012

The History Press
The Mill, Brimscombe Port
Stroud, Gloucestershire, GL5 2QG
www.thehistorypress.co.uk

British Library Cataloguing in Publication Data.
A catalogue record for this book is available from the British Library.

ISBN 978 0 7524 6590 6

Typesetting and origination by The History Press
Printed in Great Britain

Coat of Arms

City of Durham

The shield shows a white cross on a black background for St Augustine, the founder of the Church of England. The red cross represents Durham's links to the Church.

*

In 1974, as the city of Durham expanded, the arms, representing the people of the city, hold the distinctive mitre of the Bishop of Durham.

*

The two gold lions represent St Oswald, the first Christian king of Northumberland, and the miners' lamps signify the traditional industry of the region.

Contents

Durham

Pronounced /'dʌrəm/ – or locally, /ˈdʊrəm/

The name is from Old English *dun*, meaning 'hill', and Old Norse *holme*, meaning 'island'.

Dun Holm was changed to Duresme by the Normans and was known, in the Roman era, as Dunelm.

Dunelm is also the post-nominal name graduates of the university may use.

Grid Reference

Saddler Street: 54° 46′ 34.39″ N, 1° 34′ 29.24″ W

Street Names

Many of Durham's streets take the name 'gate', which is simply a Northern word for street. Not surprisingly, many street names have religious backgrounds: Hallgarth Street derives from the name of the farm of the monastery of Durham Cathedral, whilst Anchorage Terrace was the home of an anchorite, or hermit, who lived near St Oswald's church.

The ancient section of the city, which encompasses the peninsula, consists of Saddler Street, North and South Bailey; the retail section eventually gives way to the university buildings that line it.

Areas of the City

The centre, and most iconic part, of the city is the **peninsula**, which houses the cathedral and castle, many university buildings and the shopping area to the north. To most, students and locals alike, it is commonly known as 'the Bailey'.

To the east of the river lies **Elvet**, an area with a large student presence due to its proximity to the university campus and many colleges; it is also the home of HMP Durham.

The **Viaduct**, named after the railway bridge which dominates the skyline, is another predominantly student area, with rows of terraced housing.

Claypath, to the north and east of the city, is a growing area which is seeing the benefits of urban regeneration as it houses the Gala cinema and theatre complex, quality restaurants, bars and pubs and many local businesses and services.

Gilesgate is the closest predominantly-local community area to the city, just past Claypath, and again offers an array of local services, as well as an edge-of-town retail park, packed with megastores and fast-food outlets.

Framwellgate Moor and **Neville's Cross** sit to the north and south of the city respectively, and the suburbs, again, have their own local services. The Neville's Cross community is on the site of the 1346 battle of the same name, when the English successfully repelled a Scottish invasion.

Distance from

	Miles	Km
Ayers Rock, Australia	9,301.927	14,970
Brussels, Belgium	367.79	591.9
Centre of the Earth	3,975	6397
Death Valley, USA	5,069.146	8,158
Eiffel Tower, Paris	440.801	709.4
Frankfurt, Germany	537.61	865.2
Glasgow, Scotland	129.929	209.1
Hong Kong, China	5,903.026	9,500
Istanbul, Turkey	1,682.673	2,708
Jerusalem, Israel	2,391.036	3,848
The Kremlin, Russia	1,522.981	2,451
Lima, Peru	6,337.986	10,200
The moon (average distance)	238,857	84,403
Niagara Falls, North America	3,241.270	5,506
Osaka, Japan	5,752.033	9,257
Panama Canal, Republic of Panama	5,234.431	8,424
Queenstown, New Zealand	11,638.282	18,730
Reykjavik, Iceland	955.669	1,538
Syracuse, Sicily	1,458.980	2,348
The Taj Mahal, India	4,300.510	6,921
Ural Mountains, Russia	1,713.742	2,758
Vatican City, Italy	1,093.613	1,760
Washington DC, USA	3,543.059	5,702
Xanthi, Greece	1,529.195	2,461
Yellowstone National Park, USA	4,396.823	7,076
Zurich, Switzerland	798.462	1,285

Town Twinnings

Durham, North Carolina, USA

Tübingen, Germany

Kreis Wesel, Germany

Kostroma, Russia

Department of the Somme, France

Banská Bystrica, Slovakia

Nakskov, Denmark

Alcalá de Guadaíra, Spain

Jász-Nagykun-Szolnok, Hungary

Other Durhams

Durham, Ontario, Canada

Durham, Nova Scotia, Canada

Durham, Arkansas, USA

Durham, California, USA

Durham, Connecticut, USA

Durham, Kansas, USA

Durham, Maine, USA

Durham, North Carolina, USA

Durham, New Hampshire, USA

Durham, New York, USA

Durham, Oklahoma, USA

Durham, Oregon, USA

Durham, Pennsylvania, USA

Fort Durham, Taku Harbor, Alaska, USA

Historical Timeline

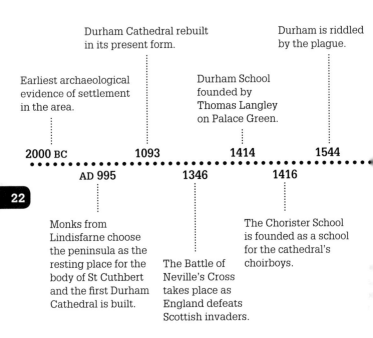

Durham Cathedral rebuilt in its present form.

Durham is riddled by the plague.

Earliest archaeological evidence of settlement in the area.

Durham School founded by Thomas Langley on Palace Green.

2000 BC   **1093**   **1414**   **1544**

AD 995   **1346**   **1416**

Monks from Lindisfarne choose the peninsula as the resting place for the body of St Cuthbert and the first Durham Cathedral is built.

The Battle of Neville's Cross takes place as England defeats Scottish invaders.

The Chorister School is founded as a school for the cathedral's choirboys.

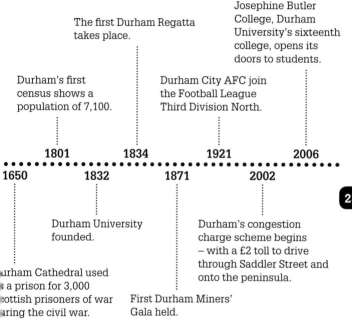

The first Durham Regatta takes place.

Josephine Butler College, Durham University's sixteenth college, opens its doors to students.

Durham's first census shows a population of 7,100.

Durham City AFC join the Football League Third Division North.

1801   **1834**   **1921**   **2006**

1650   **1832**   **1871**   **2002**

Durham University founded.

Durham's congestion charge scheme begins – with a £2 toll to drive through Saddler Street and onto the peninsula.

urham Cathedral used ; a prison for 3,000 cottish prisoners of war uring the civil war.

First Durham Miners' Gala held.

Weather and Climate

Stunning alike in sunshine or snow,
Durham beats the national averages:

	Durham	UK
Average national rainfall (ins):	25	44
Average sunshine hours (per year):	1,374.6	1,125
Frost (days per year):	52	55.6
Average daily maximum temperature (°C):	12.5	12.1
Average daily minimum temperature (°C):	5.2	5.1

A Day in the Life

0600 –   Durham University cricketers and rowers start their first session of the day.

0730 –   First Holy Communion at Durham Cathedral.

1000 –   First UNESCO World Heritage tour of the day begins at Palace Green.

1250 –   The YUM van – the mobile arm of the university's catering service – offers lunch to researchers and students alike at the School of Biomedical and Biological Science on the university's science campus.

1700 –   Last undergraduate lectures of the day at Durham University begin.

1930 –   Durham City AFC mid-week matches kick off.

2000 –   Popular entertainment at the Gala Theatre and Cinema is in full swing.

2130 –   Last admission for swimmers at Freeman's Quay Leisure Centre.

0200 –   The city's popular nightclubs close.

How Many Times a Year?

Routine services in Durham Cathedral –

1,317

Durham City AFC play at home in the league –

21

Days of Durham Regatta –

2

Festive pantomime shows at the Gala Theatre –

57

Visitors to the university's Botanic Garden annually –

80,000

Visitors to the Lumiere Festival –

75,000

Demographics

Durham city population (2003)

87,100

Male:

48.9 per cent

Female:

51.1 per cent

Birth rate:

8.9 (per 1,000)

Death rate:

9.6 (per 1,000)

Life expectancy for males:

75.1 years

Life expectancy for females:

79.9 years

Stunning Statistic

In addition to the UNESCO World Heritage Site of the cathedral and castle, Durham city contains over 630 listed buildings.

Good examples of Grade I listed buildings include:

Chorister School

St Giles' church, Gilesgate

St John's College and Chapel

Churches of St Mary-le-Bow (now the Durham Heritage Centre) and St Margaret of Antioch

Good examples of Grade II listed buildings include:

Bishop Cosin's House, Palace Green

University Library, Palace Green

Crown Court, Old Elvet

The railway viaduct

Town Hall and Guildhall, Market Place

Literary Links

The stunning landscape and surroundings mean that for many writers Durham offers a backdrop that can awaken the imagination and inspire.

> 'I got off at Durham... and fell in love with it instantly in a serious way. Why, it's wonderful – a perfect little city.... If you have never been to Durham, go there at once. Take my car.'

So wrote **Bill Bryson**, in *Notes From a Small Island*. He added:

> 'I unhesitatingly gave Durham my vote for best cathedral on planet Earth.'

Bryson eventually became the first American to become a freeman of the city, and the chancellor of the university.

C.S. Lewis was a lecturer for two years in Durham, during which time he was greatly inspired: *The Abolition of Man* began life as a lecture series at the university, and the fictional 'Edgestow' and Durham have an uncanny resemblance.

Also, take a walk along the riverside paths from Prebends Bridge to Framwellgate Bridge one evening and look out for the gas lamps lighting the way, along with criss-crossing paths. Add in snow, the river mist, and a degree of 'which path shall we take?', and you may begin to see a little of Narnia…

'To see Durham is to see the English Sion and by doing so one may save oneself a trip to Jerusalem.'

Wrote **Symeon of Durham** in *Tract on the Origins and Progress of this, the Church of Durham* in the twelfth century.

Sir Walter Scott wrote *Harold the Dauntless* after being inspired by the view of Durham Cathedral. Prebends Bridge has a stone tablet carved into it, containing lines from the poem:

'Grey towers of Durham

Yet well I love thy mixed and massive piles

Half church of God, half castle 'gainst the Scot

And long to roam those venerable aisles

With records stored of deeds long since forgot.'

GREY TOWERS OF DVRHAM
YET WELL I LOVE THY MIXED AND MASSIVE PILES
HALF CHVRCH OF GOD HALF CASTLE 'GAINST THE SCOT
AND LONG TO ROAM THESE VENERABLE AISLES
WITH RECORDS STORED OF DEEDS LONG SINCE FORGOT

Famous for...

St John's College's Just World Coffee Shop claims to be 'probably the oldest [fair-trade shop] in the world'. Founder Richard Adams went onto develop Traidcraft, who aim to fight poverty through trade and are the UK's leading fair-trade organisation.

On a darker note, Durham has had its fair share of high-profile thefts:

In 1998, a 1623 First Folio – a compendium containing the plays of William Shakespeare – was stolen from Durham University. Ten years later, antiques dealer Raymond Scott submitted it to the Folger Shakespeare Library in Washington DC, USA, asking for authentication and a valuation. Estimated to be worth up to £15 million, the Folio was in poor condition, having had its bindings removed in order to hide its provenance. Although cleared of theft, Scott was found guilty of handling stolen goods and removing stolen property from the UK and sentenced to eight years' imprisonment. In 2010, the Folio was back on display at the university before going for restoration.

A bust of Sir Ove Arup, the designer of Kingsgate Bridge, was stolen from its plinth outside the Durham Students' Union in 2006, never to be seen again. Calls from conservationists to 'bring me the head of Ove Arup' fell on deaf ears, and the bust has never been recovered. In September 2011, it was announced that Durham University had applied for planning permission for a new bust, in conjunction with the City of Durham Trust.

Mr. WILLIAM
SHAKESPEARES

COMEDIES,
HISTORIES, &
TRAGEDIES.

Published according to the True Originall Copies.

LONDON
Printed by Isaac Iaggard, and Ed. Blount. 1623.

Bond, James Bond

George Lazenby, James Bond in *On Her Majesty's Secret Service*, studied drama at the College of the Venerable Bede (now part of the College of St Hild and St Bede).

Roger Moore also attended the College of the Venerable Bede, but never graduated as he was conscripted for National Service.

A third James Bond, **Sean Connery**, is linked with Durham, in what is a mix of myth and misunderstanding. Several sources claim that, while growing up, he worked as a milkman at St Cuthbert's Society; however, it was at St Cuthbert's Co-Operative Society in Edinburgh that Connery was actually employed!

Haunted Durham

The Shakespeare Tavern on Saddler Street is the city's oldest pub and claims to be England's most haunted pub. It is a warren, with five small cosy rooms, and has a selection of real ales. Worth the ghost hunt!

Durham Cathedral supposedly has a passage to Finchdale Abbey that is so terrifying that no one can survive it, whilst a Durham Castle staircase is haunted by a wife of a former Prince Bishop: it is where she fell and broke her neck.

The ghosts are not confined to the ancient buildings: after one inmate murdered another with a knife, **Durham Prison** has a supposedly haunted cell, one which worries even the most hardened of criminals! Rumours suggest that the cell is now a storeroom…

Lumley Castle (see page 116) has spooked both the Australian and West Indian cricket teams. In 2005, Australia player Shane Watson supposedly slept on Brett Lee's floor after haunted goings on. Watson was one of several players who didn't sleep well in the castle, which is supposedly haunted by Lily Lumley, a fourteenth-century lady of the manor who apparently was thrown down a well by two priests after refusing the Church.

Five years earlier, three members of the West Indian team, including Captain Jimmy Adams, checked out of the hotel mid-stay as they were 'scared'. Next time the Windies came to the North East, they stayed in a Durham city hotel instead.

Infamous for...

Milburngate House
Constructed in the 1960s by the government, and housing both the Identity and Passport Service and the Department of National Savings and Investments, Milburngate House is on a prominent riverside site in the city, and is also the least loved (and most aesthetically awful) building constructed in a city of such architectural significance and cultural heritage.

'To Let' Boards
With the student population taking over much of the city-centre housing, every year a rush occurs as students look to secure accommodation for the next year. As such, the city becomes covered in plastic 'To Let' boards, giving an unsightly appearance to street after street. Numerous campaigns, by local people and the MPs alike, have tried to get them banned – but, as yet, with no success.

Durham City AFC's 2009-10 season was full of promise, after two successive promotions left the club just three leagues from the football league.

On the eve of the season, however, their major £1 million plus sponsor withdrew, leaving the club penniless and unable to pay their players – who promptly left! They managed to limp through the season by replacing the players with local sixth-form college students, finishing thirty-eight games later with zero points – earning them the infamy of being England's worst team that season, but gaining them much national publicity.

To make matters worse, they'd actually won two games – but had already seen six points deducted for fielding a suspended player under a false name.

Making the Headlines

In 1720, a plan was made to **make Durham a sea port**! The idea was to construct a canal to the north to meet the River Team, a tributary of the Tyne, near Gateshead. When this idea was abandoned, another plan was mooted: to make the River Wear navigable by ship from Sunderland to Durham. The increasing size of ships and the expansion of Sunderland meant the idea never came to fruition, but the statue of Neptune in the Market Place provides a reminder of Durham's maritime ambitions.

On a darker note, **serial killer Mary Ann Cotton** is inextricably linked with Durham and the surrounding area, as she moved across the region with her ever-changing family. By her execution at the age of forty, some twenty-one people linked to her had died:

Firstly, she married William Mowbray, and of eight children they had, seven died. Then William Mowbray too died, leaving Mary Ann with the insurance payments of £35.

Her second husband, George Ward, died fourteen months after their wedding. They had met whilst she was working as a nurse in Sunderland Infirmary, where he was a patient.

Next, Mary Ann married James Robinson. Overall, four children and Mary's mother died whilst they were together. Mary Ann suggested that her husband should get life assurance. He refused; they separated.

After this, in 1870, Mary Ann married again – this time to Frederick Cotton. A week later, she took out insurance on her new husband and his two sons. A year later, he was dead.

The story ends as, burdened with her last husband's sons and being pregnant with the child of a lover who refused to marry her, Mary Ann needed more work. She therefore needed someone to look after the youngest, Charles. After asking if he could be put in the workhouse without her and being refused, she reportedly said something along the lines of that 'he wouldn't be trouble for much longer'. A week later Charles was dead – finally prompting suspicion!

A doctor found traces of arsenic in his stomach. Mary Ann was arrested and other bodies exhumed, and the result was the same: every single one had traces also. On 8 March 1873, Mary Ann Cotton was found guilty on a single charge of murdering Charles, and sixteen days later was hung in Durham Prison.

Museums and Attractions

The **Durham Heritage Centre and Museum** sits on the Bailey in what was the church of St Mary le Bow. It chronicles the city from medieval times to the present day, and appeals to all ages with its centre for brass rubbings.

Durham Light Infantry Museum and **Durham Art Gallery** occupy the same building to the north of the city near County Hall. The DLI museum tells the story of the regiment from its formation in 1758. The museum includes a medal room, with original Victoria Crosses, part of a collection of 3,000 medals. Durham Art Gallery is the county's largest modern and contemporary art gallery and showcases a series of collections.

The university also runs visitor attractions open to the general public in the shape of its **Old Fulling Mill Museum of Archaeology**, based in a former fulling mill on the banks of the River Wear and overlooked by the cathedral and its **Oriental Museum**.

The fulling mill contains artefacts dating to prehistoric times, whilst the Oriental Museum, situated in Elvet Hill House to the south of the city, houses over 23,500 objects stretching from Japan and South East Asia to Egypt. It is northern Britain's only museum dedicated to the Far East.

Buildings

Durham is dominated by, and world famous for, **Durham Cathedral**. The present site has been used to house the relics of St Cuthbert since AD 995, with the construction of the present Norman building beginning in 1093 and completed in 1133.

It served as a prison for Scottish prisoners of war in 1650 for Oliver Cromwell. The cathedral's treasures include the head of St Oswald of Northumbria, the remains of the Venerable Bede and three copies of the Magna Carta from 1216, 1217 and 1225.

The central tower stands 66 metres high, and is open to the public, giving spectacular views of Durham County.

In 1986, together with **Durham Castle** (which faces the cathedral across Palace Green), the site became a UNESCO World Heritage Site.

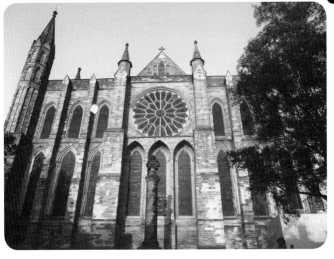

Facing the cathedral, Durham Castle sits at the other end of Palace Green, and is open to the public for guided tours, despite being a fully functioning college of Durham University.

Built in the eleventh century, the castle was donated to the university in 1837 for accommodation for students and became known as University College.

The Great Hall, although now shortened, stands 14 metres high and 30 metres long, whilst the Undercroft is a hive of student activity, serving as a common room and student bar. The Lowe Library, opened in 1925, houses over 10,000 books.

University College is the most over-subscribed college at the university: 2006 saw 2,858 applications for just 170 places.

The Market Place houses the **Town Hall** and **Guildhall**, the entrance to **Durham Indoor Market** and an array of impressive architecture.

The square and adjoining shopping streets were refurbished in 2011 at a cost of £5.25 million, in a scheme, dubbed 'Heart of the City', which has caused huge controversy over its use of 'modern' furniture in a historic setting.

The Marquess of Londonderry statue sits at the south of the square and provides one of Durham's best myths (see page 112).

With traffic a problem in the area, the city runs a congestion-charge scheme for any car entering the peninsula through the only road entrance in the Market Place, and was the first city in UK to do so, beating London by a few months.

Dunelm House, the Durham Students' Union, is regarded in the city like Marmite – it is either loved or hated!

Constructed under the supervision of Sir Ove Arup, who is responsible for the adjacent Kingsgate Bridge (and more notably for Sydney Opera House), the building is notable as it has a wide internal staircase which runs entirely straight and links all five floors in order to create the feeling of an interior street.

The building contains study space, a café and bar as well as office space for various organisations including Durham University Charities Kommittee (DUCK), which raises over £800,000 annually for hundreds of local, national and international charities.

The number of listed buildings in Durham means that regardless of which path you take, look up and around and you will see something of note.

Walking along Old Elvet, the striking red brick of **Old Shire Hall** houses many of the university's administrative departments, whilst over the road the County Marriot Hotel balcony plays host to many dignitaries, and comes to prominence during Durham Miners' Gala.

Just around the corner, the **Durham Crown Court** is striking, with its imposing pillars surrounding the entrance. Towards the river, the simple but elegant cricket pavilion of the Racecourse sports grounds and the classic design of the riverside boathouse are yet more gems.

Head to the east side of the city and you cannot fail to be amazed by the engineering of the **railway viaduct**, which dominates the area, or wander to Durham University's **observatory**, which has housed daily weather records since the 1840s, and is complete with domed roof.

The cobbled hill of **Crossgate**, complete with independent pubs and businesses such as the **pancake shop**, oozes Durham charm, whilst adjoining **South Street**, with some of the most expensive addresses in the city, offers lovingly cared for period homes on one side, and stunning castle and cathedral views on the other.

Durham has seen a number of new developments in recent years, which have greatly enhanced the city centre. The sympathetic design and architecture of these developments has added greatly to the appearance of the city and brought it into the twenty-first century.

The £19 million **Millennium Place** project houses the Gala Theatre and Cinema and Clayport Library, as well as an urban environment of shops, bars and restaurants. With a wide-open central precinct, Millennium Place has extended the city centre towards Claypath and is universally popular.

The **Prince Bishop's Shopping Centre** offers over forty shops and 400 multi-storey car parking spaces in the centre of Durham. It was designed as streets of shops rather than a covered 'arcade'.

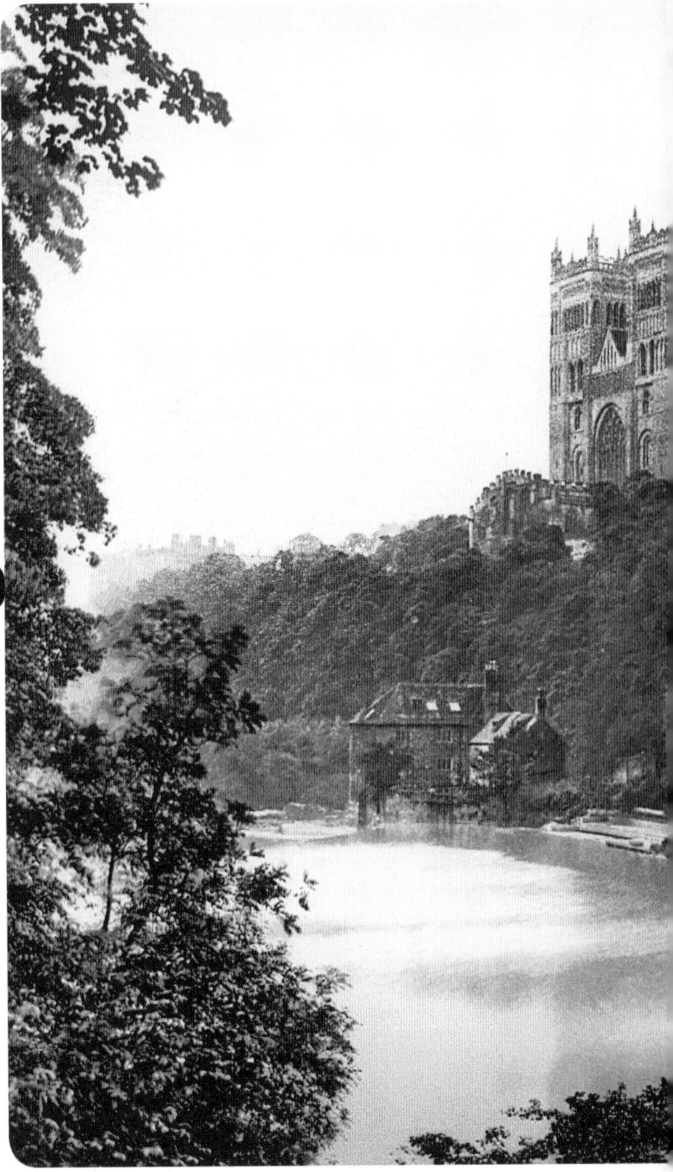

Parks

Wharton Park
To the north of the city, Wharton Park sits above the train station and offers breathtaking views across to the Bailey Peninsula. Complete with tennis courts and a Victorian-style conservatory, Wharton Park is hugely underused in the city – the students don't seem to know of its existence!

Botanic Garden
The university-owned Botanic Garden, to the south of the city, is a 25-acre site of mature woodland and attracts over 80,000 visitors annually. It houses an array of exotic plants, replicates tropical conditions in its glasshouses, and is home to a large arboretum. The visitor centre and cafeteria are open daily, and the site provides an academic resource for both teaching and research.

The Sport Complex and Palace Green
Although not strictly parks, the largest green spaces in the immediate city centre are the university racecourse sport complex and Palace Green. In the summer term, expect both to be highly populated by students.

River Wear

With its source at Wearhead and meeting the sea at
Sunderland, the River Wear gives Durham its shape and has
defined what it has become. Its meander created the high
peninsula on which the cathedral and castle sit, and provided
a strategic defensive position. Passing through Durham
city, the river has two weirs, both of which were created for
industrial activities, and is crossed by seven bridges.

In 1965, just two salmon were recorded as being caught in the
Wear. In 2010 the number stood at 1531 – putting it firmly in
the Environment Agency's top ten most improved rivers.

Rules of the River Wear, as agreed by the University Boat
Club, Durham Amateur Rowing Club and Durham School:

All boats must keep to the right-hand side.

The overtaking boat has right of way, and must move to the
centre of the river to overtake.

An overtaking crew going downstream has right of way over
an overtaking crew rowing upstream.

All crews in darkness, or likely to be on the water in
darkness, must carry lights – a white one at the bow, and red
to the stern.

Bridges

Seven bridges of differing significance cross the River Wear at Durham.

Both the Framwellgate and Elvet bridges are twelfth-century; Prebends Bridge, meanwhile, was constructed in 1777. All three are pedestrianised but, with the exception of Prebends, all are part of an access-and-delivery only scheme at night.

Kingsgate Gate, which adjoins Dunelm House, the Durham Students' Union, was opened in 1966 by Sir Ove Arup and is one of two narrow pedestrian bridges. After his death in 1988, Arup's ashes were scattered from the bridge, which he considered to be his best work. The other, Pennyferry Bridge is the newest crossing in the city: it opened in 2002, on the site where a 1d ferry used to cross the river.

The final bridges are the road bridge of New Elvet, under 100 metres away from Elvet Bridge, and Milburngate Bridge, opened in 1973, which carries four lanes of traffic and acts as part of the northern stretch of the city's small ring road.

Employment

Total Employment by Sector:

Agriculture/forestry/fishing/energy and water-supply industries:

2.2 per cent

Manufacturing:

9.6 per cent

Construction:

6.4 per cent

Services:

82.1 per cent

Socio-Economic Groups:

Higher and intermediate/managerial/professional:

23.6 per cent

Supervisory/clerical/junior management:

27.4 per cent

Skilled manual workers:

13.7 per cent

Semi-skilled/unskilled manual workers:

18 per cent

On state benefit/unemployed/lowest grade workers:

17.3 per cent

For the wider county area, tourism is one of the biggest sectors. It is estimated to be worth at least £650 million to the local county economy, brings 18 million visitors and sustains more than 12,000 jobs.

Although the county is famed for its strong industrial and coal-mining heritage, the city was largely bypassed by the Industrial Revolution, and developed instead as a centre for the Church and for academia.

As such, the third largest employer in the county is Durham University, which has an annual turnover of £150 million. It is estimated that people linked to the university (staff, students, visitors) spend another £60-70 million in the region annually.

Local people

Rowan Atkinson was born in the nearby steel-industry dominated town of Consett. The actor, of *Mr Bean* and *Blackadder* fame, attended The Chorister School, as did former Prime Minister Tony Blair.

Paul Collingwood, the ex-England cricket captain, resides in Durham and can be seen regularly in the Riverside Ground in nearby Chester-le-Street, playing for Durham CCC.

Playwright **Thomas Morton** (1764-1838) was born in the city, whilst novelist Hugh Walpole was educated in the city and based many of his books in an imaginary cathedral town.

Sir Peter Vardy was born in nearby Houghton-le-Spring and was educated at both the Chorister School and Durham School. Vardy controlled Reg Vardy car dealerships, which had been launched by his father, and sold it in 2006 for £506 million. The Vardy Foundation funded the building of four schools in the North East.

Once Bishop of Durham, **Michael Ramsey** was the 100th Archbishop of Canterbury.

Durham University

Founded in 1832 and granted a royal charter five years later, Durham University can lay claim to being the third oldest in England.

Teaching over 15,000 students, the university is run by a collegiate system, whereby every student is a member of one of sixteen individual colleges. The university owns many of the buildings in the city centre, with the law, history, theology and music departments all being housed on the Bailey and Palace Green.

Unlike at most universities, Durham students do not wear mortarboards at their graduation ceremonies. It is said this tradition dates back to 1898, when the first female members of St Hild's College graduated as full members of the university. In disgust, their graduating male counterparts abandoned tradition and threw their mortarboards into the River Wear. Since then, the only mortarboards worn at graduation ceremonies belong to the academic staff. (Though, strangely, posing in a mortarboard for the graduation photos is still an option!)

Colleges of Durham University:

Collingwood

Grey

Hatfield

John Snow (Stockton Campus)

Josephine Butler

St Aidan's

St Chad's

St Cuthbert's Society

St Hild and St Bede

St John's

St Mary's

Stephenson (Stockton Campus)

Trevelyan

University (known to many as 'Castle')

Ustinov

Van Mildert

Famous Alumni:

With a list of fame and fortune that could stretch for pages, notable Durham University alumni include:

David Bellamy OBE (botanist, author and broadcaster)

Edward (Ted) Wragg (educationalist and well-revered *Times Educational Supplement* columnist)

David Sproxton CBE (co-founder of Aardman Animations of *Wallace & Gromit* fame)

Tim Smit KBE (founder of the Eden project)

George Alagiah OBE (BBC newsreader and presenter)

Chris Hollins (BBC News sport correspondent and *Strictly Come Dancing* winner in 2009)

Gabby Logan (television presenter)

Jeremy Vine (author, journalist and news presenter)

Mo Mowlam (former politician and Secretary of State for Northern Ireland)

Sir Milton Margai (first Prime Minister of Sierra Leone)

Andrew Strauss and **Nasser Hussain** (current and former England cricket captains)

Jonathan Edwards (British Olympic Gold Medallist)

Will Carling and **Phil de Glanville** (ex-England rugby captains)

Jon Snow (broadcaster and news presenter)

General Lord Richard Dannatt (Chief of Staff of the British Army)

Favourite Scene

Least Favourite Scene

Festivals and Events

Brass, Durham's international festival, brings a range of diverse and adventurous music to Durham every year in July, and unites brass, folk, opera, dance and outdoor theatre, constantly pushing the boundaries of what brass music can be, and is perceived to be.

Durham Book Festival brings literary greats to Durham in abundance each autumn. Using a variety of venues across the city, it offers entertainment workshops and story-telling for everyone from young children to adults and ranges from formal question-and-answer sessions to informal hands-on events. One for all the family.

Lumiere, Durham's four-day annual Light Festival is one of the highlights of the year. Attracting internationally acclaimed artists, it turns the city into a stunning display of lights, illuminations and performances. Attracting over 75,000 visitors in its first year, Lumiere has grown year by year and lit up even more of the historic city centre and beyond.

Durham Beer Festival comes to the city at the beginning of September, putting it out of reach for the majority of students – which means that there are plenty of beverages to go round for all! Run in association with CAMRA, the three-day festival offers over 100 different types of beer, cider and perry.

Durham Food Festival, based on Palace Green in late October, brings together a mix of farmers' markets and Continental flair, with meats and cheeses, fine wines, cakes and fruits. Established in 2011, over 6,000 people visited in its first two days, with 'celebrity chef' cooking demonstrations and book signings complimenting over seventy-five food stalls. There are also craft and gift stalls, and many artists and poets are usually present. Expect to see it grow in the coming years.

In a city with such a grand student population, another highlight is the university's **summer graduation week**, straddled between the end of June and early July. Bringing a host of families and friends to the city, expect palatinate purple bunting to adorn the streets, outdoor table-space to be filled to the brim with jugs of Pimms and champagne, and to see the splendour of the students parading in their graduation robes and celebrating the end of their time in the city.

The king of all Durham events is the **Miners' Gala**, which attracts an international audience.

Now over 125 years old, it is the event of the Durham summer. Held on the second saturday in July, it attracts crowds of well over 100,000. Originating though the region's strong coal-mining heritage, the gala is a coming together of all the mines and collieries across the county and beyond. Although now they are all closed, their histories remain to be celebrated.

Each colliery or village marches through the city behind its banner – and with friends and family – to a mass rally held on the Racecourse, before then proceeding to a service in the cathedral. Each banner tells the story of the village it represents, from Chopwell – known locally as 'Little Moscow' for its strong Communist support – to Easington's, which has been edged in black since 1951, when a mining accident killed eighty-three men.

Expect it to bring the city to a standstill as it becomes awash with colour, noise and vibrancy – the bands will play, the Bevin Boys will sing, and the locals will remember their heritage.

Pubs

With a blend of rich historical heritage and a healthy student population, Durham has a great selection of real-ale pubs, all of which have their own unique and picturesque settings or quirky tale to tell.

The ones worth a visit include:

The Dun Cow: quirky, tiny and interesting.

The Shakespeare Tavern: allegedly the most haunted pub in England (see page 42).

The Swan and Three Cygnets: with a beer garden overlooking the River Wear.

The Victoria Inn: CAMRA recommended this as the best in Durham.

The New Inn: if you are a student…

Sport

Cricket in Durham

Before moving to their purpose-built ground in Chester-le-Street, Durham CCC played their home games at the Racecourse, one of the university's sporting grounds. The facility is still home to Durham MCCU – the university's First Eleven, who have full first-class status and play regular matches against full county sides, producing an array of international talent.

Next door to the Racecourse is the home of Durham City CC. With grass banking providing a natural amphitheatre effect and river views, both venues offer a great way to spend a few hours on a lazy summer day and drift off in the most quintessentially English way.

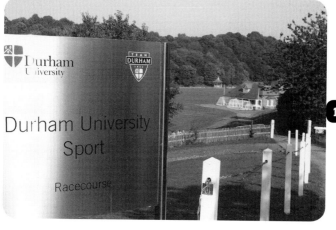

With the River Wear playing such an important historical role in the city's history and development, it is no surprise that rowing is one of the most popular sports.

The flagship event is **Durham Regatta**, which began in 1834, making it the second oldest regatta in Britain and earning it the nickname of the 'Henley of the North'. Run every second weekend in June, two different length courses are used, with hundreds of different races taking place.

Durham schools, the university and the Durham Amateur Rowing Club all use the water regularly. The first rowers of the day take to the river before sunrise and the last return to the boathouse after sunset.

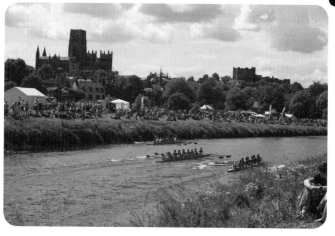

Although less prominent than in many cities, football is alive and kicking in Durham. Durham City AFC hit prominence in 2009/10 (see page 48) but the club has a long and rich history.

The 'Citizens' were members of the Football League from 1921 to 1928, playing in the Third Division North. In 1957, they reached the second round of the FA Cup, with Tranmere Rovers the opposition. The 7,000-crowd is Durham's record attendance. City now play their home games at the edge of town, in a purpose built 3,000 capacity stadium, with 300 seats and cover for a further 600 spectators, complete with a 'third-generation' pitch.

Durham City Rugby Club were founded in 1872, and play their home games at 'Hollow Drift', at the end of Green Lane. They are regarded as one of the strongest amateur teams in the county. With a good relationship with the university, ex-students Phil De Glanville and Will Carling, who both went on to captain England, have pulled on the club's navy and gold strip.

Television

As a city of such stunning architecture and scenery, Durham is a popular choice for television producers for a range of programmes.

Inspector George Gently, the BBC drama based on the 1960s' novels of Alan Hunter, has filmed many scenes in Durham, with Palace Green, the castle and university buildings being popular backdrops. Many extras are drawn from the student population.

The Tide of Life, based on the novel of Catherine Cookson, used the cathedral and surrounding area for many shots, whilst *Time Team*, and a host of natural, social and ancient history programmes, also have made use of the unparalleled delights of the peninsula.

Film

Not surprisingly, **Durham Cathedral** has been used as a film backdrop on many occasions.

Its quadrangle is often seen in the *Harry Potter* series as Harry, Ron and Hermione walk between lessons. Despite the series reaching the end, the legacy will always live on in Durham. Small clues remain of the cathedral's enchanted existence, as part of a false wall and pillar blend perfectly into the 1,000-year-old stone as a lasting reminder. The year 2011 saw the university introduce a 'Harry Potter and the Age of Illusion' course as part of its BA Education Studies programme.

It also became the Palace of Whitehall for the coronation scene in *Elizabeth*, featuring Cate Blanchett, in 1998.

Music

No busking license is required to play in the city centre, meaning on any given day, whilst wandering through the streets, you could find yourself greeted by a huge amount of buskers, all competing for your spare change.

Although it is unlikely that his career began as a busker, John Garth (1721-1810) the revered composer of *The First Fifty Psalms Set to Music* fame, hails from Durham – as does, on a more contemporary note, Gem Archer, the guitarist formerly of Oasis and now with Liam Gallagher's new band Beady Eye.

Paddy McAloon, from the band Prefab Spout, who had a top ten single in 1988 with 'The King of Rock and Roll', lives in Durham. McAloon has also written songs used by Kylie Minogue, Cher and Jimmy Nail.

Quirky Facts and Myths

The Market Square is home to the statue of the third Marquess of Londonderry on horseback – Charles William Vane Tempest Stewart. The Marquess owned many collieries around the city and also is credited with founding a harbour in nearby Seaham to act as a coal port.

Perhaps the biggest myth of the city is that surrounding its sculptor, Rapheal Monti. Legend has it that Monti claimed his work was perfection, and that it was impossible for a flaw to be found. However, it is said that a blind beggar man did what no one else had been able to do and found a flaw. After feeling the statue all over with his hands, he proclaimed (correctly) that the horse had no tongue! On hearing this, Monti was said to have committed suicide.

Despite being widely believed, it is just a story!

Durham Awards

In 2011, Durham won the following awards:

Second Best City in the UK
As voted by the *Guardian*

Durham Cathedral – 'Britain's Best Building'
As voted for by readers of the *Guardian*

Best Private Market in UK
Durham Indoor Market was awarded this honour by the
National Association of British Market Authorities

Small Visitor Attraction of the Year
For the Botanic Garden, as voted by the North East England
Tourism awards 2011, Silver Award

Attractions

The surrounding area that makes up County Durham is full of attractions that complement the city, and offer entertainment for all ages.

Beamish Open Air Museum, near Stanley, is one of North England's greatest attractions – as proved by its awards list, which include European Museum of the Year, British Museum of the Year, Best UK attraction for group visits and the Sandford award for Heritage Education. The museum is a snapshot of life in the area at the height of the Industrial Revolution and attracts over 350,000 people annually. Built with a small town, working trams, shops and houses, expect museum staff in period dress, carrying out antiquated tasks – and in some cases, waiting for willing helpers. Beamish is a significant educational tool, with many school groups using the museum, but on a 300-acre site, it can cater well for the numbers it attracts.

The nearby town of Chester-le-Street is home to the **Emirates Durham International Cricket Ground**, known locally as the Riverside, at which Durham County Cricket Club play. County Champions in both 2008 and 2009, England players past and present, such as Steve Harmison, Paul Collingwood and Ben Stokes turn out for Durham, and the quality of the ground is such that it regularly hosts England. Its crowning glory to date will come in 2012 and 2013, when it hosts an England v Australia one-day international and a five-day Ashes test.

Lumley Castle, a popular venue for weddings and conferences, but also fine dining and Elizabethan banquets, sits overlooking the River Wear and the Riverside ICG and is over 600 years old. Formerly the residence of the Bishop of Durham, it was at one time part of Durham University's University College. It was sold in the 1960s.

Penshaw Monument sits to the east of Durham between Washington and Houghton-le-Spring, and is a half-sized replica of the Temple of Hephaestus in Athens. One of the pillars contains a spiral staircase which was closed to the public shortly after the death of fifteen-year-old Temperley Arthur Scott in 1926. At the end of August 2011, the National Trust, which owns the monument, offered a special opening to members of the public. It was so popular – though only a tiny proportion of those who turned up actually made it to the top – that the Trust are now considering adding more open days in the future.

The Angel of the North is 12 miles north of Durham city, on the edge of Low Fell, Gateshead, overlooking the A1. The statue itself is 66ft tall, has a wingspan of 177ft and is made of steel. Erected in 1998, the Angel can withstand winds of over 100mph, thanks to the 600 tonnes of concrete in its base (which is sunk 70ft deep).

The Prince Bishops

'There are two kings in England, namely the Lord King of England, wearing a crown in sign of his regality and the Lord Bishop of Durham wearing a mitre in place of a crown, in sign of his regality in the diocese of Durham.'

The Steward of Anthony Bek, Bishop of Durham (1284-1311)

In the days when Durham was founded, it was virtually an independent state, ruled by a 'Prince Bishop'. The Prince Bishop's duty was not only to be head of the large diocese but also to defend against the Scots. Successive bishops in the North East had nearly all the power that the king had in the rest of England.

Their powers included:

Holding their own parliament

Raising their own armies

Appointing their own sheriffs and justices

Administering their own laws

Levying taxes and customs duties

Creating fairs and markets

Issuing charters

Salvaging shipwrecks

Collecting revenue from mines

Administering the forests

Minting their own coins

Buried in Durham

There are several high-profile burials in Durham Cathedral, with the **Venerable Bede** at the West End and **St Cuthbert** behind the high altar being perhaps the most famous. Both Bede and St Cuthbert have been the centre of much speculation over whether their remains are still intact after much movement over the centuries.

Sir Bobby Robson is buried in nearby Esh, and after his death and funeral, a huge invitation-only thanksgiving service was held at Durham Cathedral which attracted the biggest stars of the football and wider sporting world.

Things to do in Durham Checklist

Take a tour round the castle ☐

Have lunch in the Botanic Garden ☐

See Durham from the viewing area
outside the railway station ☐

Watch a game of cricket down at the Racecourse ☐

Stroll alongside the River Wear and relax in
the bandstand ☐

Hire a Browns Boat ☐

Climb the cathedral tower ☐

Drink in one of Durham's real ale pubs ☐

The Future

Durham City Vision, the partnership tasked with the regeneration of Durham, has a number of ambitious schemes for the future, including:

North Road – Regeneration of the transport interchange (bus station) and retail street to reconnect it to the city centre.

Milburngate House (see page 46) – Looks set to be vacated in 2012 as governmental department leases run out. Demolition would be favoured by almost everyone!

Old Shire Hall – The most prominent building on Old Elvet will lie vacant when the university moves its offices to the £69 million gateway project in 2012. The future use of the building is uncertain.

The £69 Million University Gateway Project – This project is transforming the entrance to the city from the south. With a huge development including a library extension, new law department, student services and administration, its cutting-edge design will breathe more life, shape and colour into the university's science campus.

Captions and Credits

All images are copyright of Charlotte Bellamy, or free of copyright (unless otherwise indicated).

65. Old Shire Hall; the imposing entrance to Durham Crown Court

67. The Railway Viaduct

69. Millennium Place

70-71. Durham Cathedral sits proudly above the River Wear (LC-DIG-ppmsc-08356)

73. Durham University Botanic Garden (Ken Bolton); Wharton Park (Roger Smith); Palace Green (Immanuel Giel)

75. The Riverside is home to a series of stunning walks

77. Framwellgate Bridge with the castle in the background; Elvet Bridge at the Durham Regatta (Tom Page)

79. Town Hall, within the Market Place; the Railway Viaduct (Brian Clark)

81. Entrance to Old Shire Hall; Dun Cow Lane, which leads to the cathedral

83. The Chorister School (Carol Rose); Rowan Atkinson (Jack Pearce)

85. St John's College; the Calman Learning Centre, South Road

87. The entrance to St Cuthbert's Society, South Bailey; the link between the university's main teaching areas, known to students as 'Cardiac Hill'!

89. 'The Eden Project' by Jürgen Matern; Jonathan Edwards (Ian @ ThePaperboy.com)

90. The Fulling Mill, with the cathedral watching over

91. A derelict foreground to Milburngate House

93. 'Lumiere' at the Fulling Mill (Tom Welch); Sir Arnold Wesker at Durham Book Festival (Simon James)

95. The author graduates, then poses with Chancellor Bill Bryson!; graduation robes of Durham University are a common sight in June

97. Durham Miners Gala 2007 (Oliver Dixon)

99. The Dun Cow, Old Elvet; The Swan and Three Cygnets, Elvet Bridge

101. The Racecourse – one of the homes of Durham University sport

103. The River Wear comes alive during Durham Regatta (kanu101)

105. Brown's Boats lined up by Elvet Bridge; New Ferens Park, Durham City AFC (Roger Smith)

107. *Time Team* (Stephen Sinfield); attention to detail on Palace Green

109. The quadrant at Durham Cathedral of *Harry Potter* fame! (Robin Widdison); Durham Cathedral (Olivier Bonjoch)

111. Gem Archer of Oasis (zero159); a busker plays on Framwellgate Bridge

113. The Marquess of Londonderry Statue in Market Square (Alan Fearon); horse's head (Gareth du Plessi3); beggar (Shaun Linnell)

115. Neptune stands in the Market Place (Clem Rutter)

117. Beamish Open Air Museum (Keith Edkins); Durham CCC (Nick Boalch)

119. Lumley Castle (Alison Stamp); Penshaw Monument (Malc McDonald); Angel of the North (David Wilson Clarke)

121. Forest view

123. St Cuthbert's Tomb (John Hamilton)

125. The courtyard in Durham Castle; Durham Castle overlooks Elvet Bridge (Albertistvan)